Creative Family Times

by

Allen & Connie Hadidian
Will & Lindy Wilson

MOODY PRESS
CHICAGO

To our dear friends,
Gary and Anne Marie Ezzo
and Jack and Kathy Tarr,
who have lovingly nourished,
challenged, and discipled us
in our pilgrimage as parents,
and without whom this booklet
would not have been possible.

And to our precious children,
Matthew and Marissa
and Noelle and Lauren,
who have made parenting
such a joy and delight!

© 1989 by
THE MOODY BIBLE INSTITUTE
OF CHICAGO

Scripture quotations, unless noted otherwise, are taken from the *New American Standard Bible,* © 1960, 1962, 1963, 1968, 1971, 1972, 1973, 1975, and 1977 by The Lockman Foundation. Used by permission.

The use of selected references from various versions of the Bible in this publication does not necessarily imply publisher endorsement of the versions in their entirety.

ISBN: 0-8024-3979-9

9 10 8

Printed in the United States of America

Contents

Foreword

God gave us two daughters, and through the years our desire has been to be faithful to that stewardship. We focused our efforts with the hope that our children would develop strong moral character. Because salvation is a sovereign act of God, no parent controls the spiritual destiny of his children; however, we can do much to cultivate the soil of our children's hearts.

Today couples are faced with a plurality of opinions on parenting. The result is often confusion and frustration. They desire to do right—but how? Overwhelmed, they feel the task of good parenting is hopeless. Many reluctantly surrender to despair, believing there is no sure way to develop spiritual sensitivity in their children.

In contrast, the experience and teaching of the Hadidian and Wilson families breathe timely encouragement. Through godly wisdom and creativity, they have proven that parents can have a positive impact on their children's relationship to God. What you read is not theoretical jargon or the product of a laboratory; rather, *Creative Family Times* is the by-product of two homes that are effectively nurturing children in God's Word.

You will find the practicality of this booklet refreshing. *Creative Family Times* leads you through the exciting journey of parenting from the time your children are infants till they are in early childhood. Application of the authors' counsel will produce spiritual development in your children as they take ownership of biblical values. Children with strong moral character will learn to integrate Christianity into every aspect of their lives, and the Hadidians and Wilsons will teach you how to help your children achieve that goal.

We know *Creative Family Times* will be a valuable help as you seek to be the best possible steward of God's precious gift—children.

May the Lord richly bless you.

Gary and Anne Marie Ezzo
Grace Community Church
Sun Valley, California

Introduction

Before our first baby was born there was only one thing we knew about parenting—that we wanted to raise happy, obedient, well-behaved, and—above all—godly children. We set out on a quest to find godly parents who had already accomplished that goal, or who were in the process of accomplishing it (and were succeeding!), so that they could discipline and instruct us in that enormous task. As we sought, God was more than faithful in directing us to persons who could be our role models and examples. We believe that God has used those people not only to put us on the proper road in biblical parenting, but also to point us in the right direction—and possibly more importantly, to pick us up and redirect us when we sometimes stumbled along the way. As we traveled along in this wonderful adventure of parenting, we incorporated certain ideas, activities, and traditions into our family life to help us accomplish our original and basic desire as Christian parents. What you will find in the following pages are the ideas that we have used and have found to be fruitful and successful. We pass them on to you with the hope and prayer that your family will benefit from them as much as our families have.

To read all of these ideas at once and to think about having them become a part of your family's daily living may seem a bit overwhelming. May we suggest that as you read you might focus on one or two activities that particularly interest you. Then get started on those ideas and leave the rest for later. When those first ideas have been established as a part of your family's normal routine, then attempt to incorporate other activities. In this way you will be setting attainable goals, for it is easier to be diligent at establishing just one or two ideas at a time. And once something has become a habit, it has a greater chance of staying with us over long periods of time. On the other hand, if you attempt many activities all at once, your energy will be divided by the pressure of trying to start too many new things; discouragement and frustration will set in, and soon after, burnout will occur—and the ideas you have started to try out will be forgotten! So think of this material as a resource tool, something that you will use not only today but in the months and years ahead as well.

As good and as helpful as these ideas are, we would be negligent if we didn't express the truth that there is nothing that we can do for our family that is more important than developing and nurturing our own walk with God. We have all heard that 80 percent of what our children learn is through our example—what we *do*, more than what we *say*. Therefore, it is imperative that our children see that our relationship with God is a thriving and growing one. The second most important thing that a parent can do for his children is to honor, respect, and love his spouse. The number one human relationship of a parent is to his mate. We have all heard the statement, "The best thing that a father can do for his children is to love their mother" (and vice versa). How true that is! We have included a section entitled "Marriage Time" to get you started in this area.

Lastly, it is of the utmost importance that you realize the advantages of incorporating the ideas in this book while your children are young. A few ideas can be started as early as infancy, and many of the others can be started with children between one-and-a-half and two years of age; *all* of the ideas can be started before a child is three years of age. (Of course, if your children are already older, start *now!*) There are several reasons why we make this point. First, we mention it because of the *ease* with which the ideas in this booklet can be incorporated into families while the children are young, as compared to the possible difficulty —due to resistance or to a lack of interest—you may find if you try to implement the ideas when the children are older. Second, we mention it because of the extreme benefit of raising children who can't remember a time when they *didn't* do these things—how easy it will be to keep in the habit, tradition, and routine of it all. Third, and most important, we mention it because of the solid foundation of faith that will be built into your young children as you incorporate into your daily routine ideas having to do with the spiritual development of your children.

As we close, we ask that God would bless you on your journey through *Creative Family Times*—may it be a rich and fulfilling one!

Note: To give you a frame of reference, here are our children's ages at the time of writing:

> Matthew Hadidian: three years old
> Marissa Hadidian: three months old
> Noelle Wilson: three years old
> Lauren Wilson: one-and-a-half years old

1

Devotional Living

Devotional living is using our everyday experiences and activities to teach our children spiritual truths. It is talking freely with our children about God and making Him a part of our everyday conversations. Just as Jesus used common objects—such as seeds and soil, pearls, and hidden treasures—to teach valuable lessons, we can use common objects and experiences as well to help our children see how God is intertwined in every aspect of our lives. Thus, simple activities such as taking a walk, watering houseplants, or listening to birds chirping become opportunities to teach children about God, His Word, His ways, and His Son.*

CHARACTER QUALITIES BUILT: God-consciousness, faith, love for God and His creation

BENEFITS OF DEVOTIONAL LIVING

1. Devotional living helps children realize that God is alive and active in the world—that He is not someone who is far away, but that He cares for them intimately and is with them always, wherever they are, whatever they are doing.
2. Devotional living develops children's sensitivity to everyday sights and sounds and teaches them to view those experiences as the creative handiwork of God—from watching the busyness of an anthill to listening to the pitter-patter of rain to admiring the beauty of flowers.
3. Devotional living develops parents' and children's ability to talk naturally with each other about spiritual truths, deepening their friendship, their faith, and their communication.

*The authors are indebted to Elise Arndt, author of *A Mother's Touch* (Wheaton, Ill.: Victor, 1983), for her insights into the topic of devotional living.

4. When parents express their faith to their children, they in turn teach their children how to express their faith.
5. When parents express their love for Jesus to their children, they confess their faith before men, which greatly pleases God (Matthew 10:32).

PREPARING FOR DEVOTIONAL LIVING

   The factor that has the most to do with determining how successful a couple is in incorporating devotional living into their family life is the strength of the personal relationship the couple has with God. As parents, we cannot be conveying spiritual insights to our children unless there is a deep and growing faith in our own heart. The greatest thing that we can ever do for our children is to develop our own intimate relationship with God, walking moment by moment in His presence, and committing our whole life to the fulfilling of His will. This commitment of our whole mind, soul, and spirit to our Heavenly Father will then naturally spill out in our words and actions throughout the day, thus beginning the process of devotional living.

THE PROCESS OF DEVOTIONAL LIVING

1. As each day dawns, it brings forth new opportunities to see God at work. However, many of those opportunities slip through our fingers because we are not *looking* for them. First, we need to be regularly praying that God would open our eyes and make us sensitive to the things around us; and second, we need to be conscientiously looking for those opportunities so that we can be relating them to our children.
2. One of the major hurdles to leap over in the process of devotional living is to view each opportunity as a chance to invest spiritually in our children, rather than as an interruption in an already busy day. Try to leave extra time throughout your day so that you are able to take a few extra minutes here and there to stop what you are doing and build spiritual awareness into your child's life. For example, if company is coming for dinner in thirty minutes and your child runs in from the backyard excited about a rainbow, you have already planned for a few extra minutes. You can stop your preparations, admire the rainbow with him, and tell him briefly about Noah, the ark, and the first rainbow. Develop a mind-set that considers these "interruptions" a blessing, not a frustration.
3. For many, verbally expressing their faith feels awkward. But the more you practice devotional living, the more natural it will become.

EXAMPLES OF DEVOTIONAL LIVING

1. Nature offers wonderful reminders of Bible stories and truths. A tree could remind you of the story of Zaccheus, clouds could remind you of Jesus' ascension and promised return, and weeds could be likened to sin in our lives, for just as weeds need to be pulled so that they don't threaten the life of the plants, so, too, our sins need to be constantly confessed before God so that our spiritual life isn't threatened. Visiting a lake could remind you of the story of Jesus walking on the water.

2. Animals can also remind you of Bible stories. When you see a donkey, you could tell the story of Balaam or the story of Jesus' triumphal entry into Jerusalem. A lamb could remind you of the first Passover, and a dove could remind you of Jesus' baptism. Visiting a zoo could be a good time to talk about Noah and the ark.

3. When doing laundry or washing dishes, talk about how you are making your clothes or dishes clean. Tell your child that in the same way our hearts are often dirty because of sin but can be made clean again by confessing our sins and having Jesus' blood wash our sins away.

4. When going to the grocery store, talk about how God provides food for you to eat. Tell your child that God has also provided food for our hearts by giving us His Word and the opportunity to talk to Him in prayer.

5. Use time spent watering plants to talk about how our hearts need to be fed just as plants do. Tell your child that just as a plant won't grow without water, so we won't grow to be like God if we don't spend time reading the Bible, praying, and learning about Jesus.

6. When folding or ironing your husband's clothes, talk about how big Daddy is and how God made him that way so that he could protect us and care for us. Talk about how much bigger God is—even than Daddy—and how He protects us and cares for us.

7. When a relative or friend has a baby, explain to your children how God formed that baby and how He knew the baby even *before* it was born (Psalm 139).

8. Admire a ladybug or a beautiful flower. Ask your child, "Who made that ladybug (or flower)?" Doing so will help solidify in your child the concept that God made everything.

9. When going out for pizza or after spending a day at an amusement park, thank God for enabling Daddy to work to earn the money that allows you to enjoy those pleasures.

10. When you hear the birds chirping outside, talk about how they are singing praises to Jesus. Tell your child how he also can praise God by his singing.
11. Express to your child what a good and loving God you have by telling him what a blessing he is, how thankful to God you are for him, and how he is a wonderful addition to your family. Make sure he knows that he is truly a gift sent down from heaven!

A BIBLICAL EXAMPLE OF DEVOTIONAL LIVING

Surely all of us are familiar with the story of how when Moses was three months old he was hidden in a basket and placed among the reeds by the bank of the Nile in order to escape Pharoah's command that all male Hebrew children were to be killed. Pharoah's daughter, Hatshepsut, found Moses and wanted to keep him as her own. However, Hatshepsut unknowingly returned Moses to his very own mother, Jochebed (and father Amran), to raise him until he was old enough to come and live at the palace. The author of a book we were reading has estimated that Moses went to live at the palace when he was only four or five years old. As we read that book, we kept thinking of how Jochebed and Amram must have felt *knowing* that they would have their son for only four or five years, and then he would be leaving them *forever* to live the rest of his days under the evil and ungodly influences of palace life. Can you imagine how *you* would feel if you knew that one of your children would be taken away from you when he or she turned four or five years old? One cannot help but think of the intensity with which Jochebed and Amram must have used those years at home to build into Moses a real love for God and for God's ways. One can only imagine how they must have used all the common, everyday items, experiences, situations, and activities of the day to make the reality of God more clear to Moses, especially in light of the fact that they didn't have the "modern conveniences" of the complete Word of God, Bible commentaries, Bible dictionaries, Sunday school classes, and Christian bookstores filled with "how-to" books to help them.

In many ways their experience was similar to ours with our children today. Most of us would agree that it seems with each passing generation that this world is getting more and more evil and ungodly. As with Moses, our children will be facing temptations and influences that most of us parents never had to. Just as Jochebed and Amram knew of the evil world into which they would be sending their son, do we realize the sinful world that our children will be facing, and are we preparing them for that world by giving them a sold foundation of faith?

We all knew the outcome for Moses. In later years when he had to choose between identifying himself with the hardships and cruelty endured by the Hebrews, or with the comforts and riches of palace life, he chose God's people. The *whole point* of this is that *100 percent* of the godly influence of his parents that so helped to shape Moses' character *all* took place before he even turned five years old! The challenge to us, and our challenge to you, is this:

1. Are we raising our children to love God with the same intensity that Jochebed and Amram must have felt as they raised Moses?
2. Are we using these early preschool years to their fullest to accomplish this task, or are we just letting the preschool years pass by?

Our prayer for you is that you will find the ideas shared in *Creative Family Times* to be as helpful, encouraging, and motivating to you in establishing a truly "devotionally living" family as they have been to us.

2

Play Time

Play time is a specified time during the day when each child has time to play by himself. If there are two or more children in the family, then each child plays in his or her own room. If two children share a room, then one child plays in the bedroom while the other child plays in another room.

CHARACTER QUALITIES BUILT: creativity, contentment, obedience (through the use of rules and boundaries)

BENEFITS OF PLAY TIME

1. Play time teaches children to play by themselves. It promotes creativity and imagination.
2. Siblings will often play better together during the day if they have played separately, too. They learn that it is a privilege to play with each other.
3. Play time is not the same as a time for playing alone observed when siblings have been separated because they were fighting while they were playing together.
4. Parents can use play time to their advantage. They can use this time to take showers, start housework, or make important phone calls. However, parents need to be careful not to abuse play time.
5. Play time is a beneficial routine to develop in children. If an emergency arises, a parent can rely on his children's play time to have uninterrupted time to care for the emergency.

SUGGESTED AGE AND LENGTH OF TIME

Play time can be started from the first few months of life with the use of a playpen. Here are suggested lengths of play time:

First few months of life: 10-20 minutes (twice a day)
When baby can sit by himself: 15-30 minutes (twice a day)
When baby starts crawling: 30-45 minutes (once a day)
By 15-18 months: 45-60 minutes (once a day)

These are only suggested times. You can slowly stretch your child's play time, but be aware that some days your child won't play as long as other days.

ADDITIONAL SUGGESTIONS FOR PLAY TIME

1. Have play time at generally the same time each day.
2. Don't have play time too close to nap time, or your child may fall asleep and throw his schedule off for the day.

IDEAS FOR INFANTS

1. Vary the location of the playpen for play time. For example, sometimes put it by the living room window, sometimes put it in the baby's bedroom, and, if the weather is nice, put it outside in the shade (where the baby can easily be checked through a window).
2. Don't fill the playpen with toys—just a few are fine.
3. If your child has a favorite blanket or toy, put that in the playpen.
4. A juice bottle and a few Cheerios or crackers will help get play time off to a good start.

IDEAS FOR TODDLERS

1. Between twelve and fifteen months of age, you can switch your child's play time to his room with a gate across his door. Before you switch to the child's room, check to make sure his room is safe (electrical outlets are plugged, lamp cords are out of reach, and so on).
2. If it upsets your child to see you during play time, have play time in a place where he can't see you but you can still easily check on him. Usually your child's bedroom is a good place. If you are implementing a play time for the first time at the toddler age, don't be surprised if at first your child cries and doesn't like it. Just start with less time in the beginning and be consistent in having a play time each day. Then build up gradually to more and more time.
3. Play time is a good opportunity to play Christian records or tapes for your child.
4. Set rules at the beginning, and, if necessary, remind your child of them each day at the beginning of play time. Suggested rules include:
   a. No bathroom breaks. (This should be taken care of before play time begins, but obviously there will be a few exceptions.)

b. No excessive talking to family members.
c. No throwing or mistreating toys.
d. No standing on the bed or furniture.
e. Whatever toys are taken out must be put away when play time is over.

TOY ROTATION

Rotating your child's toys will keep your child interested in his playthings. When a child doesn't see a toy for a month or two, he thinks it is new, and the toy proves to be exciting all over again.

To begin toy rotation, separate your child's toys into piles. The number of piles will depend on the amount of toys that your child has. Keep one pile in your child's room and box up the other piles and mark on them the dates they are to be brought out. Mark it on your calendar as well—otherwise you may forget!

SUGGESTIONS FOR TOY ROTATION

1. If your child has a favorite toy, keep it out all the time.
2. Rotate toys every four to six weeks.
3. Keep the boxes of stored toys in an accessible place or your diligence at rotating will be lessened.
4. Use the rotation plan not only for toys but for books as well.

3

Tape Time—Scripture Tapes and a Mommy and Daddy Tape

SCRIPTURE TAPES

When we put Matthew in bed for nap time and bedtime, we turn on Scripture tapes so that as he falls asleep he has the constant input of God's Word. We have found the tapes to be enjoyable learning tools and a practical way of familiarizing our child with Scripture.

CHARACTER QUALITIES BUILT: Scripture knowledge, faith, love for God's Word

BENEFITS OF SCRIPTURE TAPES

1. Scripture tapes help children gain biblical knowledge.
2. Scripture tapes help children memorize Bible verses.
3. Scripture tapes instill a love for hearing the Bible in children.
4. Scripture tapes prompt children to ask questions about what they have heard and provide an open door for parents to teach them more about God and His Word.

SUGGESTIONS FOR USING SCRIPTURE TAPES

1. Begin using Scripture tapes when your child is about one year old (although earlier is fine too).
2. Basically, two different types of Scripture tapes are available: dramatized and monologue (reading only) versions. We recommend using the monologue versions, because dramatized tapes can frighten young children.

3. Many good Scripture tapes are available. We use *The New American Standard Bible, New Testament* (Lockman Foundation), but others are also available. We also enjoy using a recording of Psalms and Proverbs.
4. When you purchase Scripture tapes, consider who is doing the reading. Is it a believer who truly loves and knows God? Or is it simply a well-known actor with a famous voice?
5. Play each Scripture tape over and over (both sides) for approximately one month. Or if one book of the Bible is on two tapes, play the entire book from beginning to end for one month. That will give your children the opportunity to become familiar with each Bible book or portion of Scripture before you move on.
6. Use only Scripture tapes at sleeptime. If you play tapes of music or stories, your children will become used to that and may not want to go back to Scripture tapes.

OTHER TAPE IDEAS

1. Prepare tapes for your children that apply specifically to the different religious holidays of the year so that they will be better prepared to understand the true meaning of an upcoming celebration. For example, put the Easter story on tape for your child and start playing it for him at naptime three or four weeks before Easter day arrives.
2. Use Christine Wyrtzen's "Critter Country" tape during the day for a fun way to help your children learn Bible verses and gain Bible knowledge.
3. To help your child learn Bible songs, during the day use "Wee Sing Bible Songs," by Pam Beall and Susan Nipp.
4. The tapes in the Agapeland Character Builders series are also enjoyable and helpful daytime tapes.

A MOMMY AND DADDY TAPE

A Mommy and Daddy Tape is a tape a father and mother prepare together for their child. Parents first need to pick out what they would like their children to learn, keeping in mind the ages and abilities of their children. The material might include Bible knowledge information (Scripture verses, godly character definitions, and Bible songs) and practical knowledge information (the A-B-C's, 1-2-3's, and a study of proper manners). Parents should make a list of what they want to include. In our home Mom does the talking and Dad does the singing. Whatever you do, it is best if both parents participate in the recording. When the tape is complete, play it daily for your child. You will be amazed at how quickly he will memorize the tape.

CHARACTER QUALITIES BUILT: knowledge, wisdom, proper manners

BENEFITS OF A MOMMY AND DADDY TAPE

1. A Mommy and Daddy Tape implants the Word of God into children.
2. A Mommy and Daddy Tape makes learning—whether biblical or practical—fun and easy for children.
3. A Mommy and Daddy Tape makes double use of a child's time. If a child listens to a Mommy and Daddy Tape during his play time (see pp. 12-14), not only will he be spending an hour or so playing with his toys, but he will also be learning.
4. A Mommy and Daddy Tape helps a child to review verses. If a child learns one new verse every other week, he may have trouble remembering verses he learned three or four months before. But if all the verses are included on the Mommy and Daddy Tape, he will review them every day.
5. A Mommy and Daddy Tape is personal. It takes into account a child's abilities, strengths, weaknesses, and needs. And children love to hear their parents' voices on tape.

SUGGESTIONS FOR MAKING A MOMMY AND DADDY TAPE

1. Begin using a Mommy and Daddy tape as soon as your child begins to talk.
2. Gear the tape for your individual child.
3. Make the tape fun by using a happy and cheerful voice.
4. Speak slowly and clearly. Your child will soon start talking along with the tape. Also, sing songs slow enough so that your child can sing along.
5. Use words of praise and encouragement. For example, after you go through the A-B-C's you might say, "Good, _____ (child's name). Now let's try again!"
6. Use your child's name often. Your child will love to hear his name on tape.
7. To aid your child's memory, repeat each item three times.
8. Use a specific sound to separate one item from the next. For example, after you have recorded 1 John 4:19, click two spoons together three times or snap your fingers twice before moving on to the next verse.
9. Use the tape as a review. Be sure to include verses, manners, the A-B-C's, and so on, that your child already knows.

10. Remember that the tape is a supplement to what is already taking place in your child's life—not a substitute for those things. Spend time with your child apart from the tape, helping him to memorize the material you have recorded—the verses, the definitions, his name and address, and so on. Include a daily review of what he has learned, even if it is as simple as reciting one verse or saying the A-B-C's.

11. The best time to play the tape will probably be during your child's daily play time (pp. 12-14).

12. Go a little beyond your child's ability. If your child can count to ten, count to twenty on the tape. If you want him to begin answering the phone in six months, include phone manners to prepare him for that step.

13. *Don't underestimate your child!* Some of the first sentences your child speaks can be Bible verses. Children are usually capable of learning (with our help) far more than we give them credit for.

14. Leave blank tape at the end of the cassette to add new items so you don't have to make a new tape each time you want to include new material.

15. Include a personal message for your child at the end of the tape, telling him how much you love him, how happy you are that he's a part of your family, and what a wonderful gift he is from God.

PLANNING A SCRIPT

The script below is an example of what a Mommy and Daddy tape might include. It was designed for a two-and-a-half year old. Your tape can be detailed, simple, or somewhere in between. Consider including the following items on your tape:

> Bible verses
> Songs
> The alphabet
> Godly character definitions*
> Numbers
> Days of the week
> Months of the year
> Your child's name, address, and phone number
> A discussion of manners:
>> "big church" manners
>> Sunday school manners
>> mealtime manners

*We recommend *A Child's Book of Character Building,* a two-volume book by Ron and Rebekah Coriell (Revell).

      polite manners
      company manners
      people manners
      obedience manners

A SAMPLE MOMMY AND DADDY TAPE

Side 1

1. Verses: What Does the Bible Say About . . .

On the tapes we introduced each verse by saying, "What does the Bible say about . . ." to make it easier for our children to integrate Bible truths into their daily lives. For example:

a. Daddy is outside mowing the lawn, and you and your child are inside fixing him iced tea. You say, "What does the Bible say about serving others?" Your child recites Galatians 5:13: "Through love serve one another." You respond by giving a concrete example of the verse: "That's right! And we're serving Daddy through love by making him some iced tea."

b. Your child has just told you a lie, and you're in his room for a time of discipline. You ask, "What does the Bible say about lying?" Your child responds with Ephesians 4:25: "Put off falsehood and speak truthfully" (NIV*). You then apply the verse to the situation that just occurred.

c. Children especially need times of affirmation and encouragement. Just as acts of disobedience bring discipline, acts of obedience and kindness should bring praise. When your children are playing together well, you might ask, "What does the Bible say about kindness?" They would reply, "And be kind to one another" (Ephesians 4:32). You then would praise them for how well they are playing together, telling them how much that pleases God and Mom and Dad. Some other examples follow:

> "What does the Bible say about who God loves?"
> "First John 4:19 says that God loves me."
>
> "What does the Bible say about obeying your parents?"
> "Ephesians 6:1—'Children, obey your parents in the Lord, for this is right.' "

New International Version.

"What does the Bible say about godly character?"
"Galatians 5:22-23—'The fruit of the Spirit is love, joy, peace, patience, kindness, goodness, faithfulness, gentleness, self-control.' "

"What does the Bible say about how we should treat others?"
"Philippians 2:3—'Regard one another as more important than [your]self.' "

"What does the Bible say about serving others?"
"Galatians 5:13—'Through love serve one another.' "

"What does the Bible say about complaining and arguing?"
"Philippians 2:14—'Do everything without complaining or arguing' " (NIV).

"What does the Bible say about how you know Jesus loves you?"
"Because Jesus died on the cross for my sins and He rose again."

"What does the Bible say about praising the Lord?"
"Psalm 135:3—'Praise the Lord, for the Lord is good; sing praises to His name, for it is lovely.' "

"What does the Bible say about kindness?"
"Ephesians 4:32—'And be kind to one another.' "

"What does the Bible say is the Golden Rule?"
"Matthew 7:12—'However you want people to treat you, so treat them.' "

Song: "Jesus Loves Me"

"What does the Bible say about where God is?"
"Proverbs 15:3—'The eyes of the Lord are in every place, watching the evil and the good.' "

"What does the Bible say about foolishness and the rod?"
"Proverbs 22:15—'Foolishness is bound up in the heart of a child; the rod of discipline will remove it far from him.' "

"What does the Bible say about wisdom?"
"Proverbs 3:15—'[Wisdom] is more precious than jewels; and nothing you desire compares with [it].' "

"What does the Bible say about becoming angry?"
"Proverbs 29:11—'A fool always loses his temper, but a wise man holds it back.' "

"What does the Bible say about how we are to respond when wronged?"
"First Peter 3:9—'Do not repay evil with evil' " (NIV).

"What does the Bible say about obeying God and trusting God?"
"Proverbs 16:20—'God blesses those who obey him; happy [is] the man who puts his trust in the Lord' " (TLB*).

"What does the Bible say about lying?"
"Ephesians 4:25—'Put off falsehood and speak truthfully' " (NIV).

"What does the Bible say about being thankful?"
"First Thessalonians 5:18—'In everything give thanks; for this is God's will for you in Christ Jesus.' "

Song: "Joy in My Heart"

"What does the Bible say about the way we should talk to each other?"
"Ephesians 4:29—'Do not let any unwholesome talk come out of your mouths, but only what is helpful for building others up according to their needs, that it may benefit those who listen' " (NIV).

"What does the Bible say about hiding our sin?"
"Proverbs 28:13—'He who conceals his sins does not prosper, but whoever renounces them finds mercy' " (NIV).

"What does the Bible say about confessing our sin?"
"First John 1:9—'If we confess our sins, [God] is faithful and righteous to forgive us our sins and to cleanse us from all unrighteousness.' "

*The Living Bible.

"What does the Bible say about forgiving each other?"
"Colossians 3:13—'Forgiv[e] each other, . . . just as the Lord forgave you.' "

Song: "Praise Him All the Little Children"

"What does the Bible say about who has sinned?"*
"Romans 3:23—'All have sinned and fall short of the glory of God.' "

"What does the Bible say about the penalty for sin?"
"Romans 6:23—'For the wages of sin is death, but the free gift of God is eternal life in Christ Jesus our Lord.' "

"What does the Bible say about how I can get eternal life?"
"John 3:16—'For God so loved the world, that He gave His only begotten Son, that whoever believes in Him should not perish, but have eternal life.' "

"What does the Bible say about what is the only way to get to heaven?"
"John 14:6—'Jesus said . . . , "I am the way, and the truth, and the life; no one comes to the Father, but through Me.' "

"What does the Bible say about what I must do to be saved?"
"Acts 16:31—'Believe in the Lord Jesus, and you shall be saved.' "

"What does the Bible say about God's wonderful gift of salvation?"
"Ephesians 2:8—'For by grace you have been saved through faith; and that not of yourselves, it is the gift of God.' "

Song: "Father, I Adore You"

"What does the Bible say about how wonderful God is?"
"Psalm 100—'Shout joyfully to the Lord, all the earth. Serve the Lord with gladness; come before Him with joyful singing. Know that the Lord Himself is God; it is He who has made us and not we ourselves; we are His people and the sheep of His pasture. Enter His gates with thanksgiving, and His courts with praise.

---

*The following group of verses is included to familiarize your child with the plan of salvation.

Give thanks to Him; bless His name. For the Lord is good; His loving-kindness is everlasting, and His faithfulness to all generations.' "

Song: "God Is So Good"

2. Alphabet: Learning the A-B-C's

Recite the A-B-C's three times, starting slowly the first time and getting faster the second and third time.

Side 2

1. Godly character

After you have presented each godly character quality, you can add specific examples from your child's life. For example, after recording a short description of obedience, say, "Obedience is when Mommy tells you to put your toys away and you respond quickly with a happy spirit."

"Patience: Waiting with a happy spirit"*
"Self-control: Doing something even when I don't feel like it"
"Wisdom: Thinking God's way"
"Obedience: Quickly doing what I am told with a happy, submissive spirit"
"Generosity: Sharing what I have with a happy spirit"
"Attentiveness: Listening with the ears, eyes, and heart"
"Love: Unselfishly meeting another's need"

Song: "Jesus Loves the Little Children"

"Honesty: Truthful words and ways"
"Responsibleness: Doing what I know I ought to do"
"Joyfulness: Being happy in the Lord, inside and out"
"Thankfulness: Being grateful for everything, and saying so"
"Contentment: Happy with what I have"
"Forgiveness: Treating someone with kindness, as though he never hurt me"
"Faith: Believing God will do what He says"

*Definitions of a godly character on this and the next page are adapted from *A Child's Book of Character Building,* a two-volume book by Ron and Rebekah Coriell (Revell).

Song: "The B-I-B-L-E"

2. Numbers: Counting from one to thirty

3. Days of the week

Song: "I Love You, Lord"

4. Months of the year

5. All about _____ (child's name): name, address, and phone number

Song: "This Little Light of Mine"

6. Manners

The outline given below is general. You will need to provide additional material, including an introduction for each new topic and words of praise and encouragement.

a. "Big church" manners

"In big church how should _____ (child's name) sit?"
"_____ should sit still in his chair."

"In big church should _____ talk?"
"No, there should be no talking."

"If _____ has a question in big church, how should _____ ask?"
"_____ should whisper."

"In big church can _____ turn around?"
"No, _____ should keep his eyes forward."

"When Mommy or Daddy tells _____ something in big church, how should _____ respond?"
"_____ should obey quickly with a happy spirit."

"When the teacher speaks in big church, how should _____ listen?"
"_____ should listen quietly and attentively."

"In big church what do we do?"
"We sing to God and worship Him. We pray. We give back to God what He has given to us through our money offerings. We learn about God by listening to the teacher and through reading our Bibles."

b. Sunday school manners

"In Sunday school how should _____ behave?"
"_____ should obey the teacher. _____ should sit still and quietly when asked."

"How should _____ treat the other children in Sunday school?"
"_____ should not touch the other children or hit or push. _____ should share the toys with the other children and be gentle and kind."

"When the teacher calls on _____ or asks _____ to do something in Sunday school, what should _____ say?"
"_____ should say 'Yes, Ma'm' if it's a woman, and _____ should say 'Yes, Sir' if it's a man."

Song: "Oh, How I Love Jesus"

c. Mealtime manners

"At the table how does _____ eat?"
"_____ eats quietly with no talking."

"If _____ wants to ask a question, what does _____ do?"
"_____ raises his hand."

"When _____ is all done, what does _____ say?"
"_____ says, 'May I be excused, please?' "

"After _____ is excused, what does _____ say?"
"_____ says, 'Thank you for the food.' "

d. Polite manners

"When _____ wants more of something, what does
_____ say?"
"_____ says, 'May I have some more, please?' "

"When someone says, 'Thank you,' what does _____
say?"
"_____ says, 'You're welcome.' "
(Practice saying "thank you" and "you're welcome.")

"Some kind words to say are: 'Excuse me,' 'Thank you,' 'You're welcome,' 'Hi,' 'Please,' 'Yes, Ma'm,' and 'Yes, Sir.' "

e. Company manners

"When company comes to our home, and they are leaving or
_____ is going to bed, what should _____
say?"
"_____ should say, 'Thank you for coming to our
home. Please come back again.' "

f. People manners

"When a friend says hi to _____, what does
_____ do?"
"_____ looks in their eyes and says hi."

"When someone asks _____ a question, what does
_____ do?"
"_____ stands still, looks in their eyes, and quickly answers their question."

"When _____ meets someone new, what should
_____ say and do?"
"_____ should look in the person's eyes and say, 'It's
nice to meet you.' "

g. Obedience manners

"What does _____ do when Mommy or Daddy calls
_____?"

"_____ responds quickly with a happy spirit and says, 'Yes, Mommy' or 'Yes, Daddy.' Let's try it."
(Practice with husband calling child's name and wife responding with "Yes, Daddy," and vice versa.)

"When Mommy or Daddy talks to _____, what should _____ do?"
"_____ should stand still and look in Mommy or Daddy's eyes."

"When _____ talks to Mommy or Daddy, how should he talk?"
"_____ should talk to our eyes with a happy voice and not a whining voice."

Song: "Only a Boy Named David"

7. Personal message to your child

4

Memorization Time

Just as adults need God's Word hidden in their hearts to help them overcome the power of evil, children also need God's Word in their hearts to help them in their battles against sin. When started young, the discipline of memorization will reap immeasurable benefits. In fact, it could be the very thing that gives a child true understanding of his need for a Savior, thereby leading him to surrender his life to Christ. And memorization will be a continual source of spiritual strength for children.

The following verses tell the benefits of knowing God's Word:

Thy word I have treasured in my heart, that I may not sin against Thee. (Psalm 119:11)

The law of his God is in his [the righteous man's] heart; his steps do not slip. (Psalm 37:31)

I delight to do Thy will, O my God; Thy Law is within my heart. (Psalm 40:8)

Let the word of Christ richly dwell within you. (Colossians 3:16)

And that *from childhood* you have known the sacred writings which are able to give you the wisdom that leads to salvation through faith which is in Christ Jesus. (2 Timothy 3:15, emphasis added)

As these verses indicate, one way to teach our children to delight in doing God's will is to have them memorize Scripture. We can help our children put on their armor against evil by giving them a knowledge of and a sensitivity to God and His Word. With this foundation, our children will be better prepared to resist sinning. For example, if your child takes a toy away from a friend, and they begin arguing, and you ask your son what happened, remembering what the Bible says about hiding sin may prevent your child from telling a lie: "He who conceals his sins does not prosper, but whoever renounces them finds mercy" (Proverbs 28:13, NIV). His Scripture memorization will encourage him to tell you the truth and ask his friend's forgiveness. The goal of memorization is for your children to begin living out the principles they are learning.

CHARACTER QUALITIES BUILT: Scripture knowledge, obedience to God, wisdom

BENEFITS OF MEMORIZATION TIME

1. Memorization helps children learn what is right (wisdom) from what is wrong (foolishness).
2. Memorization encourages children not only to obey Mom and Dad but also to obey God (our highest and ultimate objective!).
3. Memorization helps children learn about our majestic God, His wonderful ways, and His unconditional love for them.
4. As mentioned before, knowledge of Scripture can be the very thing that endears children to Christ, opens their eyes to their need for a Savior, and prompts them to ask Jesus to be the Lord of their lives.

THE KEYS TO MEMORIZATION

1. Start as soon as your children begin to talk. If your children are already older, start now!
2. Consistently challenge your children to memorize new verses or godly character qualities in accordance with their ages and abilities.
3. Review daily.

THE PROCESS OF MEMORIZATION

Of the different methods of memorization, we have found the first one listed below to be the most effective, as well as the most enjoyable. Choose whichever method suits you and your child best.

1. *Sign language.* We have memorized almost all of our verses and godly character qualities in a simplified sign language. I select a verse, choose out the main words, then put each word to a hand motion. To aid my creativity, I use a sign language book; but if the sign is too difficult I simplify it. If a word isn't included in the book, I sometimes look up a similar word and use that sign (for example, if "difficult" is not included, I use the sign for "hard"). Or often I make up a sign. (I

use *The Perigee Visual Dictionary of Signing*, by Rod Butterworth [Putnam].)

I then go over and over the verse with Matthew using the sign language. He follows along in word and action, doing the signs as best he can. Next I do only the hand motions, letting him recite the verse as he recognizes the signs. Eventually he is able to say the verse on his own.

Sign language is merely a tool to help your child memorize. Once the verse is memorized your child may or may not continue doing the hand movements.

This method seems to be the most beneficial for younger children —from the time they begin speaking to around four years of age. However, it can be a fun way for older children to learn, too.

2. *Repetition.* In the repetition method you go over and over a verse until your child is able to say it by himself. You may find it helpful to use repetition at a traditional time each day—after dinner, before bedtime, and so on.

3. *Fill in the blank.* Begin with the repetition method, then leave out a word, allowing your child to fill in the missing word before moving on (for example, "For God so loved the _____"). Then leave out a phrase, allowing your child to fill in the appropriate phrase before moving on ("For God so _____"). Do this throughout the verse until eventually your child is able to say the verse on his own.

4. *Pictorial memorization.* In the pictorial method you draw or paste pictures on a sheet of paper to represent the verse you are memorizing. You can do this word-by-word, phrase-by-phrase, or line-by-line. It can also be done in conjunction with any of the methods listed above. For example, the first sentence of Psalm 23 might be represented as follows:

"The Lord" (picture of Jesus)
"is my shepherd" (picture of Jesus with sheep)
"I shall not want" (pictures of needs that are met by God—food, clothing, a bed, a home)

If a short verse is being memorized, you can hang the picture on the refrigerator or put it on your child's bulletin board in his bedroom. If it is a longer verse or verses, you can put the pictures on construction paper and tie them together with a ribbon to make a book.

ADDITIONAL SUGGESTIONS FOR MEMORIZATION TIME

1. You should be sure to live out the principles in the verses your child is memorizing.

2. Affirmation is critical. As your child makes progress, give plenty of hugs and words of praise and encouragement. Make memorization an enjoyable activity your child looks forward to.

3. Select the main lesson that the verse is teaching and look for ways to apply it. Incorporating the truths your child is learning is the goal of memorization. Without the practice and incorporation of these truths, memorization will become a legalistic ritual. For example, if your child is memorizing Philippians 2:3—"Regard one another as more important than [your]self"—you could talk about the ways he could do that. For instance, he could let his younger brother play with a new ball first or could be quiet when his younger brother is napping.

4. Don't underestimate your child! Before two years of age most children can memorize a whole verse, and before three years of age most children can memorize a whole psalm (such as Psalm 23 or Psalm 100). Although children usually do not have trouble memorizing, parents often have trouble being consistent and diligent. If you have trouble in that area, commit it to God. Then work with your child in a spirit of joy. He will pick up from your attitude that Scripture memorization is either fun or boring.

5. Always teach the Bible reference along with the verse.

6. Don't limit yourself to memorizing Bible verses. You can also memorize godly character qualities, definitions, and Bible truths.

7. Review is critical. A Mommy and Daddy Tape (see pp.16-27) is helpful in this area. Here are some other ideas as well:
   a. *Meal times.* Place a card on your kitchen table with that week's verse. Seeing it at each meal will remind you not only to review the verse but also to *apply* the verse.
   b. *Traditional times.* Traditional times always include reviewing after devotions, before bed, or before prayer at mealtimes.
   c. *Creative times.* For example, always say a verse when getting your child into the bathtub and when getting him out, or have your child say a verse before he can get out of bed in the morning. Try saying a verse in place of times you would ordinarily say, "One, two, three, *go!*" For instance, when you push your child in a swing, hold him up high and give him a verse reference. When he quotes it, let him go. Then catch him again and repeat the process.
   d. *Child initiated times.* The real joy and reward comes when your children start saying their verses or character qualities on their own, with no prompting. We are delighted when we hear Matthew walking around the house saying verses, sitting in the bathtub quoting Scripture, or reciting God's Word in his bed when he wakes up. What joy lies ahead for you as you enter the world of memorization!

5

Sit Time

Sit time is a period of time each day (thirty minutes or so) when a child sits on a chair and quietly reads or looks at several books. This practice has many benefits for a child as well as for parents.

CHARACTER QUALITIES BUILT: self-control, patience, obedience (through the use of rules and boundaries)

BENEFITS OF SIT TIME—FOR CHILDREN

1. Sit time teaches children to love books.
2. Sit time enhances the ability children have to be alone and not always have to be entertained.
3. Sit time helps children to develop the ability to sit still and quietly in *any* situation, whether it be at mealtime, in the car, in a restaurant, in Sunday school, or at church.
4. Sit time teaches children self-control. It takes a great deal of self-control for most two-year-olds to sit quietly for thirty minutes.

BENEFITS OF SIT TIME—FOR PARENTS

The most obvious benefit of sit time is that it gives a parent thirty minutes or so of uninterrupted time to do needed tasks. Here are some ways you can use sit time:

1. Use sit time to provide uninterrupted time for dinner preparation.
2. Use sit time when you need to take a shower while your child is awake.
3. Use sit time at the hairdresser or barber while you get your hair cut.
4. When company is coming over, use sit time to keep the house clean and allow you extra time for last minute preparations.

5. When you are entertaining company, use sit time to have uninterrupted conversation with your company. (Your child can still be in the same room so that you can keep an eye on him.)
6. Use sit time Sunday mornings before church to have time to get yourself ready and do any needed tasks.

CHURCH WORSHIP

Eventually all of us will be taking our children with us into "Big Church" to worship together as a family. For those of us who decide to make this transition for our children at an earlier age, sit time is indispensable, for it is unfair to expect a child to sit quietly in a church service without advance training. This training should be done at home, *not* at church. If you train your child at home through the use of sit time, then the transition to a church service will be more pleasant for both you and your child.

THE PROCESS OF SIT TIME

1. If possible, begin using sit time between the ages of twenty and twenty-six months.
2. Use two to four books for sit time.
3. Depending on the age and ability of your child, begin with one to five minutes of sit time.
4. Give your child clear instructions as to what sit time is and what is expected of him.
5. At the beginning, practice with your child. For example, have your child sit on a living room chair with his books while you sit on the couch with your book. Let your child know when sit time is starting so he knows to follow his rules (which you have explained to him). After two minutes are up (and assuming your child has done well), give your child lots of praise and affirmation. The next day start with three minutes, and so on. Be sensitive to when you are overextending your child. For instance, if your child does well with a ten-minute sit time but struggles with fifteen minutes, then stay at ten minutes for a week or so. Then begin to build up again.
6. A suggested goal to work toward would be that by two-and-a-half to three years of age your child should be able to go approximately thirty minutes with sit time.
7. Start sit time on a chair, for if the child is seated on a couch or love seat he will be tempted to crawl back and forth, or play, which will only lead to unpleasant discipline. Try to make the introduction to and practice of sit time as enjoyable and pleasant as possible.
8. The use of a timer can be helpful, for it will let your child know exactly when sit time is beginning and ending.

9. In the training process, use sit time every day. Once your child has mastered sit time and it has become a well-established habit, you may cut back or use it only when needed (but still use it at least a few times a week to keep it a matter of routine for your child).

THE RULES FOR SIT TIME

1. No complaining when it's time for sit time.
2. No getting off the chair for any reason—not even if a book drops.
3. Only sitting on the chair is permitted—no jumping, standing, and so on.
4. No talking to or calling for Mom or Dad. (This rule must be used with discretion. If your child has learned not to abuse this privilege, then he might be allowed to call you for bathroom needs and so on. Be sure to enforce this rule from the beginning; if you don't you will defeat the whole purpose of sit time.)
5. Talking quietly to yourself or reading your story out loud in a soft voice is permitted. (Again, if this privilege is abused, then remove the privilege.)

To make the introduction of sit time easier for your child, consider working with him on no talking times. Begin with one minute, practice with him, then build up to more time. The no talking rule is wonderful for use when needed during devotions, mealtimes, church, and so on. However, do not start this practice until you are ready to enforce it.

Remember: Although your children may sit down for a half hour or so to read their books on their own, the whole point of sit time is for it to be done on *your* timetable, not theirs.

6

Prayer Time

Prayer is a vital part of our relationship to God, and one in which we can be a tremendous model and example to our children. By modeling prayer in our lives, we are at the same time teaching our children how to incorporate prayer into theirs.

We long for our children to have a sense of God's presence at all times, and some of this sense can be developed by teaching them what prayer is—a conversation between them and God. Our children can learn at an early age that God is always there and accessible to them when they come to Him in prayer.

CHARACTER QUALITIES BUILT: God-consciousness, thankfulness, concern for others

BENEFITS OF PRAYER TIME

1. Prayer time develops God-consciousness in children—the awareness that God is with them not just at church on Sundays or during family devotions but in every place no matter what they are doing.
2. Prayer time develops a thankful heart in children. As parents thank God for His material, physical, and spiritual blessings, children learn that these blessings come from God.
3. As parents pray for the needs of others outside their family, children develop sensitivity to the concerns of others.
4. Prayer time can be a wonderful time of rejoicing and marveling at God's wise and powerful ways as you record not only your prayer requests but also His answers to them.
5. As Christians, prayer is one of our most vital means of communion with our Lord. Starting a meaningful prayer time with our young children can only work to enhance their own relationship with God. Our

goal as parents is to develop in our children the ability to talk freely with God throughout the day; our *prayer* as parents is that this ability would last in our children throughout their lifetime.

SUGGESTIONS FOR PARENTS

1. Aside from your own individual prayer time, set aside time to pray together as a couple. Use this time to pray for your children, your marriage, your schedule for the day, and other requests in your family prayer notebook (see below). Praying together as a couple will reveal the deep thoughts and longings of your heart to your spouse —thoughts that often aren't expressed in daily conversation.
2. Pray for your child each night before you go to bed. When you go into your child's room to check on him, lay your hand on him and pray for him. If he wakes up, tell him that you were praying for him.
3. Pray with your child whenever you are about to leave him with a baby-sitter.

IDEAS FOR MODELING PRAYER TO YOUR CHILDREN

Our children will not be likely to incorporate prayer into their lives unless they first see it in ours. Because our children will probably not be up to see us having our own daily time of prayer or our prayer time together as a couple, it's important for them to see us praying at other times during the day. For example:

1. Pray together before meals.
2. Pray with your children before they go to bed.
3. Stop and pray when your children aren't getting along. Ask God to help them to be kind and loving to each other. Also, stop to praise God when your children are playing well together.
4. Pray with your children before they leave for school.
5. Pray after you have sinned in front of your children (lost your temper, said something unkind, and so on). Confess your sin to God and ask Him to forgive you.
6. Stop and pray when you see an accident or hear a siren. Ask God to be with the people involved.
7. Save your Christmas cards each year. Beginning in January, choose one card each day and pray for the person or family who sent the card.
8. Pray on your way to church. Ask God to prepare your heart and use the speaker.
9. Pray before you run errands or go shopping. Ask God to help your children be obedient and responsible, and ask Him to help you find

what you need. Be sure to thank Him for His answers when you're done.

10. Thank God throughout the day for the friends that came over, for the fun time you had at the park, or the chance that you had to go swimming.

11. Pray with your children whenever you are getting ready to go out (whether it is for a walk or out to lunch) and then again when you return. Thank God for the time that you spent together.

ADDITIONAL IDEAS CONCERNING YOUR CHILDREN AND PRAYER

1. Don't wait until your children are older before you start praying with them. For example, from the day your baby is born, pray out loud with him every night before he goes down. Or as soon as your baby starts eating solids, hold your baby's hands, bow your heads, and pray before each meal.

2. When your child is old enough to talk but still too young to pray on his own, try praying in phrases and having your child repeat the phrases.

3. Pray with your child after a time of discipline. Depending on his age, you could pray for him, have him repeat a prayer after you, or have him pray on his own, confessing his sin to God and asking for forgiveness.

FAMILY PRAYER NOTEBOOK

Because children are easily distracted, it is often difficult to keep them interested in family prayer time. Using a family prayer notebook will help keep your children interested in the time you spend praying together as a family.

BENEFITS OF A FAMILY PRAYER NOTEBOOK

1. A family prayer notebook helps parents pray systematically and regularly for friends and family.

2. A family prayer notebook is a good way to keep track of requests.

3. As a family looks back on how God has answered their prayers, a family prayer notebook leads them to praise God for His faithfulness and goodness.

4. A family prayer notebook helps children understand who or what is being prayed for.

FAMILY PRAYER NOTEBOOK SET-UP

1. Select a notebook to suit your family. (We use an 8 1/2 x 6 1/2 inch three-ring binder.)

2. Use one page per person or family. (We use 8 x 5 inch index cards.) On the front side of a page place a picture of the person (or family) with his name printed underneath. On the back side of the card, record prayer requests and answers.
3. Separate the pages into different sections with dividers. Various groupings could include: missionaries, spiritual leaders/our church (in this group you could include friends that are pastors and Christian school administrators), special friends, extended family, our family/our government.
4. When you are not able to cover a whole section per day, use a paper clip to mark where you left off.
5. After dinner is a good time to pray together as a family. You will already be sitting down together, making a natural transition to prayer possible.
6. You may also choose to pray for people who have written you letters. After you have written them back, put their letters in your family prayer notebook (in the inside front pocket if your notebook has one), and on the next day that you pray, include that family in your prayer time. After you have prayed for them, remove their letter from the notebook. This is a good way to pray for people you may not be praying for on a systematic basis.

7

Devotion Time—
Family Devotions

Deuteronomy 6:5-7 says, "You shall love the Lord your God with all your heart and with all your soul and with all your might. And these words, which I am commanding you today, shall be on your heart; and you shall teach them diligently to your sons and shall talk of them when you sit in your house and when you walk by the way and when you lie down and when you rise up."

Family devotions are one way for parents to teach their children about God. They are a time when the whole family is together for formal Bible teaching—"formal" in the sense that God's Word (or a book about God) is being read and discussed. Several excellent books are available that are simple enough so that devotions can be started with children at even the earliest ages.*

CHARACTER QUALITIES BUILT: faith, family unity, love for God and His Word

BENEFITS OF DEVOTION TIME

1. Devotion time helps parents familiarize their children with who God is, what God is like, and how God wants them to live. Through learning what God is like children can in turn learn how to honor and obey Him.

---

*For very young children (one- to two-year-olds), our favorite devotion book is Kenneth Taylor's *The Bible in Pictures for Little Eyes* (Moody). For older children (three- to six-year-olds), our favorite books include Kenneth Taylor's *Big Thoughts for Little People, Wise Words for Little People,* and *Giant Steps for Little People* (Tyndale) and Ron and Rebekah Coriell's two-volume book *A Child's Book of Character Building* (Revell).

2. Devotion time develops a love for God's Word in children. Since children love to be read to, parents can capitalize on that by helping them develop a love for God's Word. The Bible is full of exciting and fascinating stories that children will want to hear over and over again.
3. Parents can use devotion time for outreach and evangelism. For example, when some non-Christian friends were staying at our home, we asked their children to participate in our family devotions. The children loved to answer the questions, and within two days they already knew most of the songs. Each day they would ask if we would have devotions that night. It was a great way to share God's Word not only with the children but also with the parents, who listened along. To further the outreach, before our friends arrived we specifically picked out pages in our devotion book that spoke of Jesus and what He has done for us.
4. Devotion time builds family unity as the family spends structured time together.

WHEN TO HAVE FAMILY DEVOTIONS

Many of us only think of family devotions occurring right before bed —but that doesn't have to be the case. In order for family devotions to become a habit, they need to be at a time of day when you will be most consistent in having them. Try different times of the day to see what works best. In a family where the father works evenings, right after breakfast may be the best time, and in a family where the father leaves for work before the children get up, after dinner may be the best time.

You don't need to limit devotions to only once a day. Because our daughters love stories so much, I have some devotional time with them after breakfast, even though it is just the three of us. Now a morning doesn't go by without Noelle asking, "Mom, can we have a story?"

Some examples of incorporating devotion time into your day include:

1. Have Mom go through a character building book during the day and Dad read the Bible at night.
2. Read Bible stories (such as Adam and Eve, Noah and the ark, Daniel and the lion's den) after breakfast, and concentrate on Jesus' life and work on earth in the evening.

WHAT TO DO DURING FAMILY DEVOTIONS

1. Consider including story reading, a question time, review of memory verses, prayer time, and singing in your devotion time. The amount of time you spend will depend on your schedule for the evening. Some

nights you may spend only fifteen minutes; other nights you may spend thirty-five minutes.

2. Collect several musical instruments and put them in a "music basket." During the singing time distribute the instruments to be played as you sing. On the last song line up and march around the living room.

3. Remind your children of Psalm 69:30-31: "I will praise the name of God with song, and shall magnify Him with thanksgiving. And it will please the Lord better than an ox or a young bull with horns and hoofs." Stress the fact that they should be singing *to* God and not just making noise with their mouths. Let them know that their singing pleases God.

4. Variety is the key to keeping devotions fun.

   a. Vary the amount of time you spend on each part of devotions. For example, try singing the whole time, or if Dad is usually the only one who prays, have everyone in the whole family pray, or try spending the majority of devotion time reviewing verses and talking about what they mean and how they can be practically applied.

   b. Vary what you do during devotions. For example, act out the story yourselves or with puppets, or use a flannel graph board. Try having a different family member lead devotions.

   c. Vary what you're studying about during devotions. Read through the Bible from beginning to end, read Bible stories, talk about developing character qualities, or study Jesus' life and ministry or Bible truths.

5. Involve your children in devotions. While telling the story (or afterwards) ask questions to make sure your children understand what you are teaching. For younger children, have them point to different items in the picture that are relevant to the story. The more they can participate, the more enjoyable it will be for them.

ADDITIONAL SUGGESTIONS FOR FAMILY DEVOTIONS

1. Use family devotions as a time to teach self-control. Set rules for devotion time that include sitting still with hands to yourself, listening quietly while the story is being told, and so on.

2. Set a goal of having family devotions three to five times a week. If devotions are held less than three times a week, they will probably be difficult to establish as a habit. If you set a goal of more than five times a week, you may find it too difficult to attain and quit in frustration.

3. Although it is preferable that both parents be present, don't skip devotion time because one parent is absent.

8

Bible Study Time

In our home, Matthew's Bible study time takes place during the last ten to twenty minutes before his bedtime. All of his bedtime needs have been taken care of first (devotions done, teeth brushed, prayers said, and so on). He then gets in bed, we give him his Bible, we leave the room, and Matthew "reads" and studies his Bible.

CHARACTER QUALITIES BUILT: love for God and His Word, Scripture knowledge, discipline (to regularly be in the Word)

BENEFITS OF BIBLE STUDY TIME

1. Many adults enjoy daily devotions but struggle with establishing it as a habit. Bible study time establishes this practice at a young age—one that will hopefully stay with children throughout their lives.
2. Children learn more about God and become more familiar with His Word as they study and read by themselves. Parents can then take the stories and Bible characters that they read about and further teach them the truths and principles conveyed.
3. Sometimes it is difficult for children to go from a busy day of work and play to the quietness of bedtime. Bible study time gives children a transition period to calm down and relax before the lights are turned out.

SUGGESTIONS FOR BIBLE STUDY TIME

1. *The Picture Bible* published by David C. Cook is a good Bible to use for children who cannot read.
2. When your child is about two years old, devote a whole family night to purchasing his own Bible. Go to a Christian bookstore and let him

pick out his own Bible and a special bookmarker to go with it. (Decide which Bible you want him to have in advance. Then show him two or three of the same Bible and let him choose which one he wants.)

3. While your child is still in a crib, give him his Bible study time as a ten-minute sit time (see pp. 32-34) during the day. Then when you transfer him to a regular bed, you can give him a Bible study time at night as a special privilege.

4. Establish the rule that once your child is in bed he may not get out for any reason (unless he asks Mom or Dad and receives permission).

5. For the first week or two that you are incorporating Bible study time, set a timer for ten minutes to help your child become accustomed to the new practice. Later you can end the time whenever Mom or Dad is ready for talk time (see pp. 44-45).

6. When Bible study time is over, ask questions such as, "What did you study?" or, "What did you learn tonight?" Even if your child can't read, he will learn to recognize the stories and the people by the pictures.

7. Sometimes sit next to your child in his bed and read stories to him for Bible study time. This will familiarize your child with the pictures of the Bible stories and characters so that he can recognize them when he "reads" on his own.

8. Never make Bible study time a "you-will-or-else" activity. Give your child the option of whether or not he wants Bible study time. But if you make the alternative lights out for bedtime, Bible study time will be happily chosen 99 percent of the time!

9

Talk Time

Talk time is a special time parents set aside each day to spend a few minutes alone with each child to find out how he or she is doing. In our home, we do this with Matthew at bedtime, after the lights have been turned out. (We rotate which parent does this.) Many nights talk times result in a good time of communication and fun, but other times deep needs and thoughts are brought out in the open.

CHARACTER QUALITIES BUILT: openness, parent/child friendship and trust

BENEFITS OF TALK TIME

1. Talk time strengthens the parent/child relationship.
2. Establishing a talk time assures that parents do not get too busy to spend a few quiet moments alone with each child. (Parents with more than two children can rotate this so that each child gets talk time every other night.)
3. Although the questions that parents ask at talk time should be asked at other times of the day also, there is something about the atmosphere of talk time—the child anticipates its coming, he is all snug in bed, Mom or Dad is at his side, the lights are out—that creates for a child a needed platform to share his thoughts and feelings, which may be too personal to tell during the day.
4. If talk time is established as "routine" in the younger years, and the children feel a real freedom to share during this time, it can only serve to help parent/child communication as the children grow into their teen years.

IDEAS FOR TALK TIME

A good time to begin talk time is when your child makes the transition from his crib to a regular bed. The following are some ideas of the types of questions or statements to bring up during talk time:

1. How was your day?
2. What did you do today?
3. Is there anything that happened today that Daddy (Mommy) needs to know about?
4. What would you like to talk about?
5. How do you feel inside? (One night, at two-and-a-half years old, Matthew responded to this question by saying, "Mommy, I'm sad inside because there is sin, and I need you and Daddy to spank me when I sin to drive out the foolishness so I can be happy." I often wonder what would have happened had I not taken the time to ask Matthew this. Would he have shared it on his own?)
6. I love God because . . .
7. Let's talk about Jesus! (This statement has resulted in questions such as, "Mommy, how do I get to heaven?" and, "Why did Jesus die on the cross?")

10

Question Time

Question time is a good way to help lessons learned in devotions and Bible study time stay with a child. Parents should not only work hard at teaching their children, but they should also work hard at helping them remember what they have learned. In our home, question time was an outgrowth of our Bible study time and devotion time. We chose the Bible question we wanted Matthew to know and then taught him the answer. For example, as we traveled on our vacation we were talking about Jesus' life and what He did for us. We taught Matthew the answers to the questions "What are the four gospels?" (Matthew, Mark, Luke, and John) and "What does 'gospel' mean?" (the good news that Jesus died on the cross for my sins and rose again).

CHARACTER QUALITIES BUILT: Scripture knowledge, love for God and His Word, wisdom

BENEFITS OF QUESTION TIME

1. As children get to know each Bible story and Bible character through question time, they will be getting to know God better.
2. As question time progresses, children will often ask their parents questions related to *their* questions. For example, a child who is taught the answer to the question "Who built the ark boat?" might ask, "Why did God tell Noah to build the ark boat?"
3. Children will begin asking their parents *their* questions. For example, Matthew often asks, "Mommy, who led the people of Israel into the Promised Land?" When I answer the question correctly, Matthew gets excited and says, "*Good*, Mommy!"—the same as I do with him. This shows that a child is learning the questions well, not just the answers.

4. Question time is an enjoyable way of reviewing past lessons as well as helping children remember biblical facts.

1. Keep track of your child's questions and review a few of them daily.
2. The keys to a successful question time are plenty of praise and affirmation and daily review. Also, don't move on to a new question until the last one is known well.
3. You may want to incorporate a certain time of day for review. Try having question time right after talk time (see pp. 44-45).
4. Take advantage of opportunities to review questions (for example, when you are riding in the car, when you are waiting in the doctor's office, or when you and your child are fixing lunch or eating lunch together).

EXAMPLES OF QUESTIONS

The following list of questions was developed for a two-and-a-half to three year old:

1. What is the first book of the Bible? Genesis.
2. Who was Eve married to? Adam.
3. Who was Ruth married to? Boaz.
4. Who brought the house down? Samson.
5. Who tricked Samson? Delilah.
6. Who made the ark boat? Noah.
7. Who was in the lion's den? Daniel.
8. Who went from Ur to Canaan? Abraham.
9. Where was Jesus born? Bethlehem.
10. Who were Jesus' parents? Joseph and Mary.
11. Who was Abraham's son? Isaac.
12. Who was Isaac's son? Jacob.
13. Who defeated the Midianites with three hundred men? Gideon.
14. Who persecuted the Christians and then became one? Paul.
15. Who was sold into slavery by his brothers? Joseph.
16. Who led the people of Israel into the Promised Land? Joshua.
17. Who was swallowed by a big fish? Jonah.
18. What did Moses say? "Let my people go!"
19. What did the king say? "No!"
20. But the tenth time the king said . . . ? "Yes!"
21. Who built the Temple? Solomon.
22. Who killed Goliath? David.
23. Who was David's son? Solomon.

24. On what mountain did Moses receive the Ten Commandments? Mount Sinai.
25. Who returned to Jerusalem to rebuild the wall? Nehemiah.
26. Who denied Jesus three times? Peter.
27. Who betrayed Jesus? Judas.
28. Who was the son of encouragement? Barnabas.
29. What are the four gospels? Matthew, Mark, Luke, and John.
30. What does 'gospel' mean? The good news that Jesus died on the cross for my sins and rose again.
31. What city did Jonah go to? Nineveh.
32. What's the last book of the Bible? Revelation.
33. What prophet told the people of Israel to rebuild the Temple? Haggai.
34. In what year? 520 B.C.
35. Who was in the fiery furnace? Shadrach, Meshach, and Abednego.

11

Church Time—Getting Ready for "Big Church"

Children eventually reach the day when they no longer go to the nursery during church but attend the worship service with their parents. For most children, sitting quietly for long lengths of time does not come naturally. Proper training requires effort and sacrifice on the part of the parents. The benefits in the long run, however, will be well worth the effort, as parents not only train their children how to behave during church but also teach them how to participate in worship.

CHARACTER QUALITIES BUILT: self-control, love for God and His Word, worshipfulness

BENEFITS OF CHURCH TIME

1. If the training for "big church" is started at home before the transition occurs, a child's introduction to the worship service will be much easier and happier for all involved.
2. If parents try to train their children to sit quietly in the church setting, the children will likely associate any needed disciplinary action with church and the worship of God. Because parents want their children to look forward to church—not to dread it because they receive a spanking every Sunday for not behaving properly—they need to prepare beforehand by doing the necessary training at home.
3. Christian parents desire to have Sunday be the best day of the week, for the worship service to be enjoyable and meaningful. Church time offers some ideas to help accomplish that.
4. The ultimate goal in having children in the worship service is that the Sunday morning worship service will be a time for them to learn more

about God and how to worship Him. The result will be the building of a solid foundation for their own personal faith in God.

PREPARATION AT HOME

Before attending the first worship service:

1. Have sit time (pp. 32-34) well mastered at home.
2. Explain to your child what church is, what will take place there, and what is expected of him. Spend a few weeks building up to his first attendance.
3. Prepare a "big church bag" for your child—a special tote bag for him to carry to church. Include in it his notebook (see below), his Bible, a few small Christian books, and an offering wallet or purse.

BIG CHURCH TIME

1. Before the church service begins, take care of any bathroom needs. If there is time, allow your child to run outside for a few minutes (especially if he has been sitting in Sunday school for the last hour). Before going into the sanctuary, review the rules and behavior that are expected.
2. When your child first begins attending the worship service, sit in the back of the sanctuary near an aisle (for a quick exit if necessary). You may move forward as your child's behavior allows. If possible, sit where your child can see the front without having to stand. Have your child participate as much as possible during the service.
   a. *Ideas for singing time.* To promote participation on the child's part, do not make other books or papers available to him during the singing. When the congregation stands to sing, sit or kneel by your child so that he can follow along. Have your child hold one side of the hymnbook to help him feel as though he is participating and to help him from wandering down the aisle, out in front, etc.
   b. *Ideas for Scripture reading.* During the Scripture reading, help your child find the passage in his own Bible so that he can follow along as the leader reads, or share your own Bible with him.
   c. *Ideas for the offering.* During the offering, allow your child to give some of his own money that he has brought from home. One family we know has three jars for their children to keep money in—one for Jesus, one to save, and one to spend. On Saturday evening, the child chooses some money from his or her "for Jesus" jar and puts it in a special wallet or purse used only on Sundays. When it is time for the offering, he gets his money from his wallet (which has been kept in his "big church bag") and puts it in the offering plate as it is passed around.

d. *Ideas for the sermon time.* During the sermon, allow your child to read or look at his Bible or other Christian books. We highly recommend *The Picture Bible* (published by David C. Cook) for children who cannot read.

Include a small notepad or assemble a special notebook to be used for taking "notes." Use a small three-ring binder notebook to fit your child's size. Tie two or three colored pencils to the binder with string to avoid frequent dropping. Each Sunday add two or three blank pieces of paper to the notebook for that day's "notes." You may also choose to allow your child to look at his Sunday school papers during this time.

3. If your child is only staying through the first half of the service, walk your child to children's church, taking a minute to review his church behavior. Keep it short and simple but do give lots of affirmation if your child has done well or, if necessary, point out areas that need improving and ask how he could do better next time. This review is especially profitable when you are first training.

If your child has stayed with you during the entire service, review his behavior after church before too much time has passed (for example, on the way home from church or at lunch that day). Be sure to give lots of praise when he behaves well. You may wish to give a reward when appropriate, remembering that rewards are given *because* of obedience and not as a way to *get* obedience. If things could have been better, ask your child how he felt he behaved and discuss ways to improve. Also, be sure to review that day's sermon with your child, asking him what he heard and learned.

SUGGESTED GUIDELINES FOR BIG CHURCH TIME

1. The eyes should be kept forward—no turning around or staring at people behind you.
2. Only sitting is permitted (except when the congregation is instructed to stand).
3. Sit quietly with no excessive fidgeting or wriggling.
4. Resting a head on Mom or Dad's lap or shoulder is permitted, as long as there is no bobbing up and down or constantly changing from one seat to another.
5. No talking. If a question needs to be asked, whisper.
6. No getting off the seat without permission.
7. When someone is leading in prayer, the head must be bowed and the eyes closed.
8. Once something falls on the ground (book, pencil, and so on), it cannot be used the rest of the service.

Rules are not effective unless they are enforced. Regardless of whether or not your rules are the same as those suggested above, a few exits from the service will more than likely be inevitable. For this reason do not start "big church" time until you are ready to discipline your child for improper behavior.

ADDITIONAL SUGGESTIONS FOR "BIG CHURCH" TIME

1. Alternate Sundays (if possible) for which parent is in charge, so one parent is freed up to worship and listen intently.
2. When your child is very young (two-and-a-half to five years old) you may wish to give him the option of attending the entire service with you or of going to children's church after the first half of the service.

12

Mom (or Dad) and Me Time

One of my greatest desires for my children is for them to not only view me as their parent but also as one of their dearest friends. A good way to cultivate that friendship is to do fun things with them. That's why mom and me time was started at our home. For some parents, playing with their children for extended lengths of time comes naturally. They can let their dishes, dusting, or unmowed lawns wait while they play with their kids. For others of us, play time doesn't come so naturally. It's easy to try to get one more chore done or one more errand run rather than seizing that opportunity for fun time with our children.

CHARACTER QUALITIES BUILT: parent/child friendship, creativity, imagination

BENEFITS OF MOM (OR DAD) AND ME TIME

1. Mom (or dad) and me time is a fun time that is scheduled, thereby ensuring that time spent playing with children is not missed.
2. This fun time encourages a strong bond of unity between parent and child, something especially needed today.
3. Through their choice of activity, the parents can expand their children's horizons, whether it is in the area of art, cooking, woodworking, or exploration of God's creation.

SUGGESTIONS FOR MOM (OR DAD) AND ME TIME

1. Schedule a mom (or dad) and me time one or two times per week. This is not meant to be the *only* time when you play with your children; it is to be used as a time to do special projects that you wouldn't do every day (for example, a special craft project or a picnic).

2. Because mom (or dad) and me time is different from your children's normal play time, it will require advance planning. One mom I know plans her mom and me time two to three months in advance. The advantage of this type of scheduling is that you only have to take one day to plan and make only one trip to the craft store to buy all the necessary supplies. Another option is to plan weekly. The advantage to planning weekly is that you can center your activities around what your child is learning at that time, what he enjoys, what the weather is like, and so on.

3. Sometimes make mom (or dad) and me time pure fun—finger painting, going to the park with a picnic lunch, and so on; other times relate the time to a spiritual truth or Bible story that you are currently learning. For example, build a wali out of Popsicle sticks when you are learning about Nehemiah and how he rebuilt the wall around Jerusalem; or make a collage out of leaves, flowers, pebbles, and twigs when you are studying about God's creation. Sometimes stay at home and do crafts; other times go to interesting places.

IDEAS TO DO AT HOME

Listed below are various ideas to do at home, materials to have on hand, and different projects to make. These ideas can be used not just for mom (or dad) and me times but for other times as well.

1. *Finger painting.* Finger paint with shaving cream, hand lotion, whipped soap flakes, pudding, or tempera paint (mix tempera with liquid starch).
2. *Play dough.* Use cookie cutters and a rolling pin with play dough (make your own with the recipe below).
3. *Dough art.* Make Christmas ornaments out of dough (see recipe below).
4. *Modeling clay.* Make shapes out of modeling clay and either bake or air dry.
5. *Straw painting.* Dribble paint onto paper and blow into interesting designs with a straw.
6. *Vegetable printing.* Cut vegetables (potatoes work well) into shapes, dip into paint, and print on paper (makes great wrapping paper).
7. *Sponge painting.* Cut sponges into shapes, dip into paint, and print on paper.
8. *Tissue paper collage.* Paint a sheet of paper with liquid starch and cover with cut tissue paper; then paint again with starch.
9. *Watercoloring.* Try using watercolor as a wash over a crayon drawing.
10. *Crayon rubbing.* Place an item (such as a leaf) under paper and color over it with the side of a crayon.
11. *Chalk drawing.* Color with colored chalk on wet paper.

12. *Wax paper picture.* Sandwich objects (paper, leaves, or grated crayons) between two pieces of wax paper and iron at low setting so that the paper melts together.
13. *Woodworking.* Provide wood scraps, nails, and a hammer—and be sure to supervise!
14. *Cooking.* Let children help measure, pour, stir, and eat. Try making cookies, brownies, pudding, or lemonade.
15. *Easel painting.* Paint outdoors on homemade or purchased easel with tempera paint.

MATERIALS TO HAVE ON HAND

plastic tablecloth	crayons	tissue paper
drop cloth	chalk	shaving cream
smocks	watercolors	modeling clay
glue or paste	paint brushes	old sponges
tape	colored paper	glitter
children's scissors	straws	tempera paint
cookie cutters	cream of tartar	liquid starch

PROJECTS TO MAKE

1. *Art smock.* To protect your child's clothing, make a smock from Dad's old shirt (cut off the tails and wear backwards) or from heavy-duty vinyl (such as Naughahyde), which can be found in most fabric stores. Cut material to fit your child, leave the back open, and sew ties at the neck.
2. *Easel.* Make an easel out of a discarded wallpaper book. Turn the wallpaper book upside down and set it in a shallow box in which you have cut diagonal notches. Glue a couple of clothespins to the top of the book to hold the paper, and wipe down the easel after each use.
3. *Flannel board.* Cover a piece of lightweight wood (masonite works well) with heavy flannel or corduroy. Cut several pieces of felt in different shapes and colors to use.
4. *Sand box.* Fill a large box or tray with sand (available at most garden shops). Play in the sand with measuring cups, funnels, colanders, pails, shovels, and so on. You may also fill your box with cornmeal, salt, or water.
5. *Sewing cards.* Make your own sewing cards by punching holes in cardboard or styrofoam meat trays. Sew with shoelaces.
6. *Play dough.* Make your own with this recipe:

1 cup flour	1 T. vegetable oil
½ cup salt	2 tsp. cream of tartar
1 cup water	food coloring and extract (peppermint works well)

Mix all ingredients and cook in an electric skillet or saucepan on medium heat for three to five minutes until a ball forms. Knead until stickiness is gone. Store in an airtight container or plastic bag.

7. *Dough art.* You can also make dough art with the following recipe:

3 cups flour	1 cup water
1½ cups cornstarch	1 T. dry mustard
1 cup salt	

Mix together and knead for ten minutes. Shape, then bake at 325-350° (about one half hour per quarter-inch thickness of dough). Watch closely and brush with egg yolk during baking. The dough can be painted and then sprayed with a clear gloss spray.

8. *Rainy day box.* Make a rainy day (or 5:00 P.M.) box. Cover a large box with contact paper and fill with the following items:

crayons	sticker books	building toys (such
coloring books	stickers	as Legos or
collage items	watercolors	wood blocks)
ink pad	scissors	play dough
ink stamps	glue or paste	cookie cutters
colored paper	stencils	

13

Family Time

Family time is a time set aside (preferably one night each week) when a family spends time together participating in planned activities. The activities can vary from playing a board game to going out for ice cream to acting out a Bible story—being together as a family and relating with each other is the goal.

CHARACTER QUALITIES BUILT: family unity, family friendship, cooperation

BENEFITS OF FAMILY TIME

1. Family time is a time when the whole family is together. Times together as a family are easy to plan when children are young but become increasingly difficult to schedule as children grow older. Therefore, establishing the tradition of family time when children are young is important.
2. Family times should be enjoyable! Some evenings may be more fun-oriented than others, but it is important to include an enjoyable element in each family time. Because children learn through play, be creative in thinking of ways to teach biblical truths through fun activities. (The *Christian Family Activities* series by Wayne Rickerson [Standard] can be of great help in this area.)
3. Family time should be a time when the family participates in an activity together. Children should be active participants, not just spectators —it is their night! Gear your activities to your child's level so that he can be actively involved.
4. Today parents hear a lot about the negative influence of peer pressure. When children have as much (or more) fun with their families as they do with their friends, the impact of peer pressure is lessened.

SUGGESTIONS FOR FAMILY TIME

1. Make family time a top priority—otherwise it may end up being little more than a good intention. Pick dates two to four weeks in advance so that you have actual dates set as opposed to "seeing if you have time this week."
2. Family times don't need to be long. They can be an extended devotion time (see pp. 39-41) with fun additions. Usually thirty to forty-five minutes of concentrated time is plenty for younger children.
3. Be flexible. Try different approaches and learn what works best with your children. What you choose will vary with the ages of your children, how many children are in your family, what your family enjoys doing, and so on.
4. Family times work best when someone takes the responsibility of planning them. (For example, you and your spouse can each plan two family times a month, or you can plan them together and designate who will be in charge of having supplies ready for that night.)
   a. Plan your family time before the actual day arrives. The time will be more enjoyable if you're not frantically preparing for it.
   b. You may prefer to plan a whole month's activities (or more) at once to have plenty of time to purchase needed materials. Again, see what works best for you and what helps you to be the most consistent.
5. Out of four family nights a month, plan at least one of those as a family *day*—a whole day (or the best part of it) devoted to some activity: a picnic at the park, going to a ball game, visiting far-away friends, or going hiking.
6. Try to end each evening with a food snack. Our children have loved it! Often it's just popcorn, but each time we serve the snack on a special tray with special napkins, and they think it's great!

DIFFERENT TYPES OF FAMILY TIMES

Listed below are different ideas showing how you can vary the emphasis of each family time.

1. *Spiritually oriented.* Make Noah's ark, act out a Bible story with finger puppets, use a flannel graph board, or act out Jesus' birth.
2. *Service oriented.* Bake a batch of cookies to take to a sick friend or weed an elderly person's yard.
3. *Holiday/special day oriented.* Make Valentine's Day cards, make a birthday banner or special gift for Grandma's birthday, or plan an "Honor Dad Night."

4. *Project oriented.* Make a puzzle, clean out the garage, build a model airplane, or work on your daughter's doll house.
5. *Season oriented.* In spring, plant a flower or vegetable garden; in the summer, go camping in your backyard; in the fall, take a nature hike; in the winter, teach your children how to cut snowflakes from white tissue paper, or walk around your neighborhood to look at the Christmas lights; and so on.
6. *Fun oriented.* Go out for ice cream, go to the park, play ball in your backyard, go swimming, bicycling, or play board games.
7. *Child oriented.* Take turns letting each of your children pick the menu and the activity for the evening. Buy an inexpensive gift for him to open.

Most children don't mind what you do as long as they can do it with you. The goals of every family time should be for spiritual truths to be taught informally through relating with each other as a family and for your children to have fun no matter what you choose to do!

14

Marriage Time—Planning Meetings and Date Nights

The following ideas are meant for Mom and Dad alone. They are designed to strengthen the marriage relationship and build husband/wife unity.

MARRIAGE QUALITIES BUILT: husband/wife friendship, unity, and working together as a team

PLANNING MEETINGS

A planning meeting is a time each week when a husband and wife sit down together to plan out and review their schedule. A planning meeting takes only fifteen to twenty minutes and will prove invaluable.

BENEFITS OF PLANNING MEETINGS

1. Planning meetings help give priority to date nights and family nights.
2. Planning meetings guard a family's schedule and remind parents of birthdays, appointments, upcoming events, and things they need to do (such as find a baby-sitter, buy a wedding present, and so on).
3. When a husband and wife know each other's schedule they will feel as though they are working together as a team. They can pray more effectively knowing what their spouse has planned—an important luncheon, a pressing deadline, or a big test. Each spouse can support the other more fully when he or she knows what the other is doing. For example, a spouse can bring flowers home on a night when company

is coming, make a special breakfast for a big day, or call home after a doctor's appointment.

4. A planning meeting is also a time for parents to evaluate their overall schedule to see if they are getting too busy and need to postpone an event or, on the other hand, if it is a good time to have company over or plan an outing.

SUGGESTIONS FOR PLANNING MEETINGS

1. Meet every week at the same time to avoid forgetting, postponing, or overlooking planning meetings.
2. Plan your schedule two to four weeks in advance, and review what is coming up in the future.
3. Plan a family night and date night either weekly or every other week.
4. If your weekly calendar is too full—or if you have a difficult time saying no—cross out a night or two each week to stay at home. When someone calls you to invite you to another meeting, head up an activity, or to lead a Bible study, you can look at your calendar and honestly tell the person, "Sorry, I already have a commitment that night." That is one practical way to guard your time with your family.

DATE NIGHTS

Date night is a night when husband and wife spend some time together enjoying each other's company. Some date nights can be for serious talking, others for just plain fun, but the important thing is that you're spending time together, just the two of you.

BENEFITS OF DATE NIGHTS

1. God's plan for the family is that the husband/wife relationship be the priority human relationship. Children are a blessing from God but are not to take priority over a spouse. It's easy for parents to recognize that priority in their hearts, yet in their actions oftentimes communicate a different priority. A couple can get so caught up in meeting the needs of their children that unintentionally they neglect one another. A regularly scheduled date night can help to make sure that marriage relationships are lovingly attended to, nurtured, and cared for.
2. Sometimes intending to spend an evening together can end up being just that—a good intention. A regularly planned date night assures that couples have uninterrupted time together.

3. Date night provides an atmosphere for the sharing of deep thoughts and needs between husband and wife—conversations that aren't always possible in the presence of young children and with constant chores to do, telephone calls to make, and errands to run.

SUGGESTIONS FOR DATE NIGHTS

1. Schedule a date night at least every two weeks (once a week is preferable). If your budget is restricted or if baby-sitters are difficult to find, try planning an evening out every other week and an evening at home on the alternate weeks.
2. Take turns planning the date night. When it's the husband's turn, he is responsible for all the plans (even getting the baby-sitter), and vice versa when it's the wife's turn.
3. Be creative, and follow two rules. First, anything goes—even cleaning out the garage as long as you're together! Second, you must do what your spouse has planned. But let love dictate! For instance, don't plan on teaching your husband to knit unless he has shown an interest or plan an evening at the baseball stadium if you know your wife hates sports!
4. If your spouse works at night or arrives home late in the evening, try planning date mornings or date lunches instead (hire a baby-sitter and meet your spouse near his work at lunchtime).

IDEAS FOR DATES AWAY FROM HOME

go miniature golfing	go bowling
go out to eat	go hiking
go bike riding	have a cookout at the beach
go ice skating	visit friends
go roller skating	take a train ride to a nearby city
have a picnic at the park	go to the zoo
go fishing	go shopping
go to a ball game	go out for dessert
play tennis	visit a local museum

IDEAS FOR DATES AT HOME

cook together	do gardening
play games	do a project together
look at photo albums	read a book together
listen to music	talk (see questions listed below)
have a romantic dinner	write an encouraging letter to someone

SUGGESTED QUESTIONS TO DISCUSS AS A COUPLE

1. How has God used your spouse in your life?
2. How can various areas of your marriage and home life be directed more toward the glory of God?
3. What has been the most enjoyable time in your marriage? the hardest? the most meaningful?
4. What are some ways that you would like to change?
5. What are some ways that you would like your spouse to change?
6. How have you seen each other change and grow over the past months or years?
7. What are some of your dreams for the future?
8. How has God used your friends to help you?
9. What is one thing that you could improve in your marriage this next week?
10. How has God used marriage to change you?
11. What traits in a couple you admire would you like to have in your own relationship?
12. What are some traits that you do not want to have in your relationship?
13. What are some of the ways that your spouse brings you joy?

Moody Press, a ministry of the Moody Bible Institute, is designed for education, evangelization, and edification. If we may assist you in knowing more about Christ and the Christian life, please write us without obligation: Moody Press, c/o MLM, Chicago, Illinois 60610.